Start Testing Your Vocabulary

Peter Watcyn-Jones

Illustrated by Sven Nordqvist

PENGUIN BOOKS

PENGUIN BOOKS

Published by the Penguin Group
27 Wrights Lane, London W8 5TZ, England
Viking Penguin Inc., 40 West 23rd Street, New York, New York 10010, USA
Penguin Books Australia Ltd, Ringwood, Victoria, Australia
Penguin Books Canada Ltd, 2801 John Street, Markham, Ontario, Canada L3R 1B4
Penguin Books (NZ) Ltd, 182–190 Wairau Road, Auckland 10, New Zealand

Penguin Books Ltd, Registered Offices: Harmondsworth, Middlesex, England

First published in Sweden by Kursverksamhetens förlag 1982
Published in Penguin Books 1985
10 9 8 7

Made and printed in Great Britain by
Hazell Watson & Viney Limited
Member of BPCC Limited
Aylesbury, Bucks, England
Set in Times

INTRODUCTION

Owing to the emphasis in recent years on functional and communicative approaches to language learning, many other important areas of the language have been neglected. One such area is vocabulary. This series is an attempt to remedy this situation not only by filling a real gap in the materials available but also by attempting to show that vocabulary learning can be just as much fun and just as stimulating as other activities. There are five books altogether in the series, ranging from Elementary level to Advanced. Each book contains fifty tests or exercises and, to facilitate self-study, a key is also included. Students using these books should find vocabulary learning both stimulating and enjoyable and, hopefully, start to develop a real sensitivity to the language.

Start Testing Your Vocabulary is the first book in the series and is intended for Elementary students. It aims to build up a basic vocabulary of approximately 700 words which are arranged, where possible, into familiar areas such as jobs, food, sports and hobbies, the home, parts of the body, and so on. Since the student's range of vocabulary at this level is not very wide, there is a strong emphasis on drawings and approximately half the tests are picture-based. Other techniques employed are gap-filling exercises, crosswords, choosing the appropriate word or antonym, one-sided dialogue writing plus others equally stimulating and imaginative.

TO THE STUDENT

This book will help you to learn a lot of new English words. But in order for the new words to become "fixed" in your mind, you need to test yourself again and again. Here is one method you can use to help you learn the words:

1. Read through the instructions carefully for the test you are going to try. Then try the test, writing your answers **in pencil**.
2. When you have finished, check your answers and correct any mistakes you have made. Read through the test again, paying special attention to the words you didn't know or got wrong.
3. Try the test again five minutes later. You can do this either by covering up the words (for example, in the picture tests) or by asking a friend to test you. Repeat this until you can remember all the words.
4. **Rub out your answers**.
5. Try the test again the following day. (You should remember most of the words.)
6. Finally, plan to try the test at least twice again within the following month. After this most of the words will be "fixed" in your mind.

CONTENTS

1 Missing verbs 1

Fill in the missing verbs in the sentences below. Choose from the following (see example):

swim	write	drink
dance	sleep	cry
read	run	laugh
sing	drive	listen

1 They say that people from Wales can ....*sing*....... very well.

2 I feel very tired today because I didn't .... very much last night.

3 I don't like going to the beach with my friends because I can't ....

4 I always .... to the news on the radio in the morning.

5 Do you .... to work or do you go by bus?

6 It's no good asking John to waltz – he can't ....

7 I don't like babies; they .... too much!

8 I think I'll stay in tonight and .... some letters.

9 I like Dave Allen very much. He's so funny. He always makes me ....

10 We usually .... champagne on New Year's Eve.

11 I always .... the newspaper before I go to work.

12 I find it hard to .... these days. I really must stop smoking.

2 Opposites 1: adjectives

Write down the opposite of each of the words on the left. Choose from the words on the right (see example):

ADJECTIVE	OPPOSITE	
1 good	*bad*	closed
2 fat		new
3 big		poor
4 tall		bad
5 full		dry
6 young		slow
7 open		short
8 wet		thin
9 hot		low
10 old		cold
11 happy		empty
12 fast		soft
13 high		small
14 rich		sad
15 hard		old

3 The face

Write the numbers 1–15 next to the correct words (see example).

eye	....	forehead	....	nose	....
mouth	....	chin	....	eyebrow	....
tongue	*12*	ear	....	lip	....
hair	....	cheek	....	teeth	....
eyelash	....	jaw	....	freckles	....

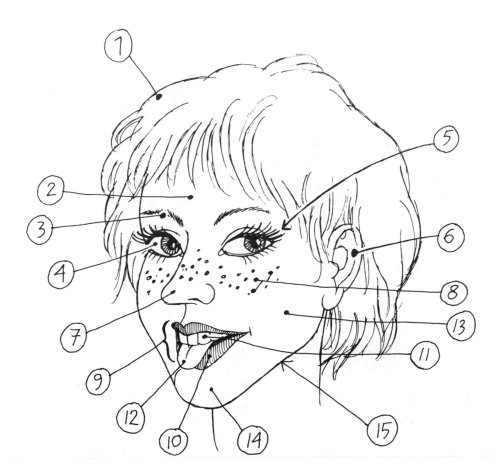

4 Prepositions of place

Look at the drawings and fill in the missing prepositions in the sentences below. Use each of the following once only:

in	through	inside
on	in front of	under
next to	opposite	outside
behind	over	between

The post office is

.... the

bank and the library.

The lion is

.... the cage.

The cat is

.... the bed.

The car is parked

.... the phone box.

He is standing

.... a tree.

The bridge is

.... the river.

The book is

.... the table.

The dog is lying down

.... the fire.

The flowers are

.... a vase.

The cinema is

.... the restaurant.

There's a man

.... the window.

They walked home

.... the park.

5

5 Missing verbs 2

Fill in the missing verbs in the sentences below. Choose from the following (see example):

learn	open	ask
carry	phone	watch
eat	sit down	play
fly	wash	smoke

1 Could you ....*open*........ the window, please? It's very hot in here.

2 It only takes a few hours to .... from London to New York by Concorde.

3 Could you .... the theatre to find out what time the play starts tomorrow night?

4 Did you .... the film on television last night?

5 How long did it take you to .... to play the guitar?

6 "Would you like a cigarette?"
"No, thank you. I don't ...."

7 Could you .... this bag, please? It's too heavy for me.

8 I'm tired. Can't we .... for a minute?

9 I don't think I'll go out tonight. I want to .... my hair.

10 If you don't know the way in England you can always .... a policeman.

11 Do you know how to .... bridge?

12 I never .... meat. I'm a vegetarian.

6 The body

Write the number 1–15 next to the correct words (see example):

arm ....
toe ....
chest ....
head ....
back ....
shoulder ....
foot ....
finger ....
elbow ....
hip ....
knee ....
hand ...8...
neck ....
leg ....
buttocks/ ....
backside

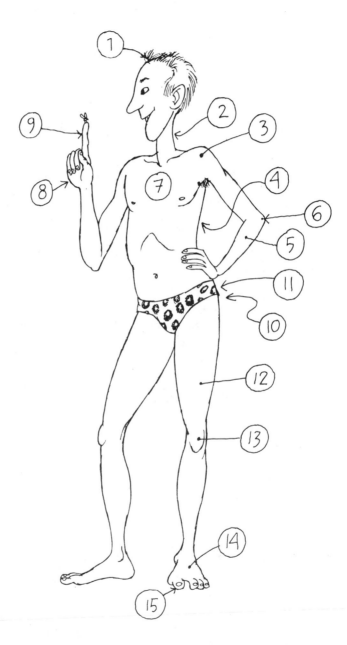

7 Missing verbs 3

Fill in the missing verbs in the sentences below. Choose from the following (see example):

climb	know	sell
shut	forget	wear
come	tell	walk
cook	spell	lose

1 Would you like to ...... *come* ...... to my party on Friday?

2 Excuse me, do you .... the way to the station, please?

3 I live very near my office, so I usually .... to work.

4 Can you .... me what time the film starts, please?

5 Shall I .... my blue dress or my red dress to the party?

6 "Could you .... your name, please?" he asked.

7 .... the window, please. It's cold in here.

8 Did you ever .... trees when you were a child?

9 I think I'll .... my car and buy a motorbike instead.

10 My wife always gets very angry if I .... our Wedding Anniversary.

11 Not many men know how to .... (At least that's what they say to their wives!)

12 I hate playing cards with my wife because I always seem to ....

8 Opposites 2: more adjectives

Write down the opposite of each of the words on the left. Choose from the words on the right (see example):

	ADJECTIVE	OPPOSITE		
1	right	*wrong*		thin
2	strong			unkind
3	dead			expensive
4	early			unfriendly
5	thick			awake
6	wide			stupid
7	male			wrong
8	kind			late
9	clever			difficult
10	clean			narrow
11	cheap			noisy
12	easy			weak
13	friendly			dirty
14	quiet			alive
15	asleep			female

9 Countries and nationalities crossword

Fill in the following crossword. Each answer is a country or a nationality.

DOWN ↓

1 He is British. He comes from ...
2 She is Italian. She lives in ...
3 He comes from Sweden. He is ...
4 They are Dutch. They come from ...
5 He was born in China. He is ...
6 We come from Greece. We are ...
7 He is German. He was born in ...
8 She is Danish. She comes from ...
9 Mr and Mrs Carter come from the USA. They are ...

ACROSS →

1 She is Swiss. She comes from ...
2 He is Polish. He was born in ...
3 My girlfriend is ... She was born in France.
4 He comes from India. He is ...
5 They come from Norway. They are ...
6 He was born in Russia. He is ...
7 She is Spanish. She comes from ...

11

10 Jobs 1

Write the number of each drawing next to the correct word(s).

a postman	....	an electrician	....	a doctor	....
a policeman	....	a typist	....	a nurse	....
a shop assistant	....	a secretary	....	a dentist	....
a waiter	....				

11 Missing verbs 4

Fill in the missing verbs in the sentences below. Use the Present Simple (*work, works, finish, finishes, etc.*) in sentences 1, 3, 4, 8, 10, 12. Choose from the following (see example):

copy	count	cut
draw	finish	follow
hear	help	leave
look at	speak	understand

1 My wife starts work at 9 o'clock and .... *finishes* .... at five.

2 She can't .... you, I'm afraid. She's deaf.

3 What time does the next bus ...., please?

4 Janet is very clever, isn't she? She .... at least six different languages.

5 The teacher asked the class to .... the blackboard.

6 My son has only just started talking but he can already .... up to ten.

7 Put the knife down! You might .... yourself!

8 Samantha always .... the way I dress.

9 Would you .... me to move the piano, please?

10 I think James is going to be an artist. He .... so well.

11 "................................... me, please," the guide said to the group of tourists.

12 I don't speak English very well but I .... quite a lot.

12 Choose the word 1

Fill in the missing word(s) in each of the following sentences (see example):

1 Would you like .... *some* .... more tea?
   (a) some   (b) any   (c) have

2 I .... German quite well, but my wife can't.
   (a) am speaking   (b) can speak   (c) can

3 My husband .... in London.
   (a) is born   (b) are born   (c) was born

4 One of my hobbies .... golf.
   (a) are   (b) is   (c) were

5 My brother is very .... He's at least 190 cms.
   (a) tall   (b) high   (c) long

6 Do you know how .... it is from London to Manchester?
   (a) long   (b) much   (c) far

7 I got this book from a very good friend ....
   (a) of me   (b) to me   (c) of mine

8 .... likes John. He's very popular.
   (a) Everyone   (b) All people   (c) Nobody

9 What time do you usually .... in the morning?
   (a) get up   (b) raise   (c) go up

10 I didn't see you at the party, Sarah. Were you ....?
   (a) sick   (b) bad   (c) ill

11 Can I .... your phone, please?
   (a) borrow   (b) use   (c) lend

12 Can you .... me the time, please?
   (a) say   (b) tell   (c) speak

13 There aren't .... apples left.
   (a) some   (b) no   (c) any

14 .... I'm late.
   (a) Excuse me   (b) Sorry for   (c) I'm sorry

13 Jobs 2

Write the number of each drawing next to the correct word(s).

an actress	a hairdresser	a businesswoman ....
a bus driver	an office worker	a mechanic ....
a fireman	an engineer	a bank clerk ....
an optician		

14 What's the weather like?

Write under each of the drawings below what the weather is like. Choose from the following:

It's raining	It's cloudy	It's frosty
It's snowing	It's sunny	It's clearing up
It's windy	It's freezing	
It's foggy	It's thawing	

1 ....

2 ....

3 ....

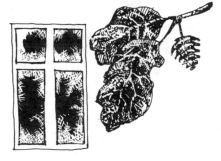

4 ....

5 ....

6 ....

7 ....

8 ....

9 ....

10 ....

15 Missing verbs 5

Fill in the missing verbs in the following sentences. Use the Present Simple (*knock, knocks, etc.*) or the Present Continuous (*am/is/are knocking, etc.*). Choose from the following (see example):

lie	shine	choose
wait	deliver	dream
pronounce	marry	cause
stay	knock	make

1 David! I think someone ......*is knocking*...... at the door!

2 I get very annoyed when people .... my name wrongly.

3 Now that the sun .... at last let's go down to the beach.

4 Smoking .... lung cancer.

5 We always .... at the Grand Hotel whenever we visit Brighton.

6 I find it hard to believe that some people .... for money instead of love.

7 "Do you know who .... the winner of the Poetry Competition this year?"
"Yes. It's Miss Belcher."

8 Hastings is a famous town which .... on the south coast of England.

9 "What's happened to the boy who usually .... our groceries?"
"Oh, he's on holiday this week."

10 If you just .... a moment, I'll see if Mr Barlow is free.

11 This is a dress I .... for Jennifer. Do you like it?

12 One of the most famous songs in the world is "I ....
of a White Christmas".

16 Plurals crossword

Fill in the following crossword by giving the plurals of the words below:

DOWN	ACROSS
1 city	1 mouse
2 bus	2 potato
3 woman	3 child
4 glass	4 goose
5 leaf	5 foot
6 tooth	6 day
7 lady	7 man
	8 knife
	9 box

17 Food and drink 1

Write the number of each drawing next to the correct word(s).

a cup of tea	....	a banana	....	oranges	....
vegetables	....	bread	....	toast	....
an ice-cream	....	wine	....	bacon and eggs	....
jam	....	sausages	....	cheese	....

18 Opposites 3: verbs

Write down the opposite of each of the words on the left. Choose from the words on the right (see example):

	VERB	OPPOSITE		
1	to stop	*to start*		to take
2	to laugh	....		to turn off
3	to open	....		to dislike
4	to come	....		to borrow
5	to work	....		to depart
6	to bring	....		to start
7	to learn	....		to answer
8	to lend	....		to push
9	to turn on	....		to close
10	to ask	....		to teach
11	to like	....		to cry
12	to sell	....		to play
13	to pull	....		to go
14	to sit down	....		to buy
15	to arrive	....		to stand up

19 Prepositions of time

Fill in the missing prepositions in the following sentences. Use these prepositions:

AT (4 times)   ON (3 times)   IN (5 times)   FOR (3 times)
SINCE (twice)

---

1 What do you usually do ......*at*..... the weekend?

2 Would you like to come to my party .... Friday?

3 Mrs Green will be away .... 3 weeks.

4 I usually finish work .... 4 o'clock .... the afternoon.

5 We got to London .... 9 o'clock.

6 English children usually open their presents .... Christmas morning.

7 My husband often works late .... night.

8 Beethoven was born .... the 18th century.

9 I haven't seen Janet .... last May.

10 English children have 6–7 weeks' holiday .... the summer.

11 We are going to Italy .... two weeks .... July.

12 I first visited Paris .... 1975.

13 We drank champagne .... New Year's Eve.

14 I haven't been to the cinema .... a long time.

15 I've been a teacher .... 1967.

20 What are they saying? 1

Look at the drawings and fill in the missing words. Choose from the following:

a After you!

b Look out!

c How do you do.

d Excuse me, please.

e A box of matches, please.

f Bless you!

g Do sit down.

h Help yourselves.

i Cheers!

j Oh, sorry!

21 Missing verbs 6

Fill in the missing verbs in the sentences below. Use the past tense (*jump, jumped, want, wanted, etc.*) in numbers 2, 3, 6, 10 & 11. Choose from the following (see example):

jump	dress	move
need	rain	talk
want	clean	continue
cost	describe	enjoy

1 If you .... *need* .... any help with the washing-up, just let me know.

2 "The windows look a bit dirty, darling."
"But I only .... them yesterday!"

3 I was only three when my parents .... from London to Wales.

4 How much does it .... to hire a car for the weekend?

5 "Sandra .... well, doesn't she?"
"Well, so would you if your husband was a millionaire."

6 Björn Borg was so happy when he won the match that he .... over the net.

7 "Can you .... the man you saw outside the bank, Sir?" the policeman asked.

8 We'll stop now, but we'll .... after lunch.

9 I'm just going down to the shops, Mum. Is there anything you .... me to get you?

10 Thank you for a wonderful evening. I really .... it.

11 Last summer we went to Ireland for our holidays. The people were nice but the weather was terrible – it .... nearly every day.

12 Could you come here a minute, please, Janet? I want to .... to you.

22 Food and drink 2

Write the number of each drawing next to the correct word(s).

tomatoes	....	soup	....	a cake	....
a cup of coffee	....	beer	....	potatoes	....
butter	....	pears	....	apples	....
meat	....	a boiled egg	....	biscuits	....

23 Choose the word 2

Fill in the missing word(s) in each of the following sentences:

1 .... a strange man outside the house.
   a There's   b It's   c He's

2 I .... to Spain in the summer.
   a am going   b think to go   c goes

3 I usually go to .... at 7.30.
   a my work   b my job   c work

4 .... me the salt, please.
   a Pass   b Reach   c Hold

5 My son plays tennis very ....
   a good   b great   c well

6 How many .... were there at the party on Saturday?
   a people   b persons   c guests

7 There's a park at the .... of my house.
   a back   b backside   c behind

8 Let's have a bottle of wine .... the meal.
   a to   b with   c for

9 Do you mind if Brenda .... us to the cinema tonight?
   a comes with   b follows   c follows with

10 Shall we go for .... this afternoon?
   a a bath   b a swim   c bathing

11 Oh, sorry!

   ....
   a You're welcome.   b Not at all.   c That's all right.

12 We had .... beautiful weather last weekend.
   a so   b such   c such a

13 I'd like ...., please.
   a a loaf of bread   b a bread   c one bread

14 Did you have a .... time at the party?
   a funny   b fun   c nice

24 Today, yesterday, etc.

Look at the following calendar, then fill in the missing words in the sentences below. Choose from the ones on the right (see example):

MAY

Mon	Tues	Wed	Thurs	Fri	Sat	Sun
		1	2	3	4	5
6	7	8	9	10	11	12
13	14	15	16	17	18	19
20	21	22	23	24	25	26
27	28	29	30	31		

this morning
last night
the day after tomorrow
next Thursday
tonight
yesterday
tomorrow afternoon
last Thursday
this afternoon
tomorrow
today
the day before yesterday

1 *Today* .... is Thursday.
  (May 16th)

2 I'm getting married ....
              (May 17th)

3 I went to London ....
              (May 15th)

4 Are you going to Sally's party ....?
              (May 23rd)

5 I'm going to the theatre ....
              (7.30 p.m./May 16th)

6 My parents are coming to see me ....
              (May 18th)

7 I'm going to Manchester ....
              (1 p.m./May 17th)

8 My sister came to see me ....
              (May 9th)

9 Shall we play tennis ....?
              (2 p.m./May 16th)

10 There was a good film on television ....
              (8.30 p.m./May 15th)

11 I got a letter from my brother ....
              (8.30 a.m./May 16th)

12 I bought a new car ....
              (May 14th)

25 Food and drink 3

Write the number of each drawing next to the correct word(s).

nuts	....	a grapefruit	....	spaghetti	....
beans	....	crispbread	....	Danish pastries	....
a sandwich	....	crayfish	....	fish and chips	....
a hot dog	....	chicken	....	a glass of milk	....

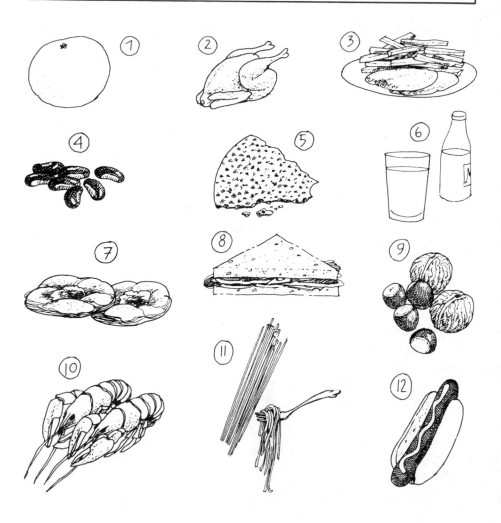

32

26 Opposites 4: more verbs

Write down the opposite of each of the words on the left. Choose from the words on the right (see example):

VERB	OPPOSITE	
1 to love	*to hate*	to mend
2 to wake up		to feel well
3 to live		to go to bed
4 to blow		to take off
5 to get up		to find
6 to spend		to hate
7 to break		to lose
8 to shout		to forget
9 to win		to save
10 to feel ill		to sink
11 to lose		to whisper
12 to show		to fall asleep
13 to remember		to suck
14 to put on		to hide
15 to float		to die

27 How do they look?

Look at the drawings below, then fill in the missing words. Choose from the following (see example):

happy	nervous	worried
sad	frightened	comfortable
ill	cold	correct
hot	tired	embarrassed

She looks *happy* He looks .... It looks ....

He looks ....

She looks ....

He looks ....

He looks ....

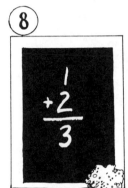

It looks ....

He looks ....

He looks ....

He looks ....   He looks ....

28 Complete the dialogue

In the following dialogue, the part of the customer has been left out. Put in the words she speaks in the right order. Choose from the following:

- Yes, that looks nice. How much is it?
- Yes, it was perfect. I'll take it.
- Yes, please. I'm looking for a jumper.
- Thank you. Now, where's my purse ...
- Er ... size 38, I think.
- Yes, please.
- Yes. Blue, if possible.
- I see. Thank you.

Shop assistant Can I help you?
Customer ....
Shop assistant I see. What size, please?
Customer ....
Shop assistant Any particular colour?
Customer ....
Shop assistant Well, what about this one?
Customer ....
Shop assistant £12.99. Would you like to try it on?
Customer ....
Shop assistant The changing-room's over there.
Customer ....
     (She tries it on)
Shop assistant Well, did it fit?
Customer ....
Shop assistant Right. I'll just wrap it up for you.
Customer ....

29 The house 1

Write the numbers 1–12 next to the correct words.

door	garden	hedge	drainpipe ....
gate	garage	wall	window ....
roof	chimney	path	balcony ....

30 Missing verbs 7

Fill in the missing verbs in the sentences below. Use the past tense (*study*, *studied*) or the Perfect tense (*have/has studied*). Choose from the following (see example):

study	bake	explain
agree	happen	decide
quarrel	fail	comb
join	demand	promise

1 I .... *baked* .... two cakes yesterday afternoon.

2 "Why aren't Mary and John talking to each other?"
  "I don't know. Maybe they ...."

3 Peter was very disappointed when he .... his driving test.

4 By the way, Julie and I .... to get married.

5 I .... French for six years at school, but I can't speak a word now.

6 It should be a good party – both David and Alan ....
  .... to come.

7 I .... to him why I wouldn't be able to come to the meeting.

8 I .... the Rugby Club two years ago.

9 A very strange thing .... to me on my way to work this morning.

10 The little girl always cried when her mother .... her hair.

11 We .... to meet outside the station at 10 o'clock the following morning.

12 The man walked into the shop and .... to see the manager.

31 Shops, etc.

Write down where you would go to in order to buy or do the things on the left.
Choose from the places on the right (see example):

YOU WANT	GO TO THE	
1 a pair of shoes or boots	*shoe shop*	florist's
2 medicine, make-up		post office
3 fish, a crab		boutique
4 sausages, meat		optician's
5 a haircut (men)		shoe shop
6 potatoes, apples		chemist's
7 butter, cheese		barber's
8 whisky, wine		baker's
9 a bunch of roses		dry-cleaner's
10 a newspaper, a magazine		stationer's
11 cigarettes, matches		fishmonger's
12 a loaf of bread, cakes		grocer's
13 stamps		furniture shop
14 a new hair-do (women)		ironmonger's
15 a sofa, a bed		launderette
16 the latest fashion		butcher's
17 a ring, a watch		off-licence
18 to clean a jacket or a skirt		hairdresser's
19 a hammer, a screwdriver		café
20 a new pair of glasses		greengrocer's
21 to cash a cheque		jeweller's
22 to do the weekly washing		travel agency
23 a cup of tea, a sandwich		newsagent's
24 to book a holiday		bank
25 a pen, envelopes		tobacconist's

32 The house 2

Write the numbers 1–15 next to the correct words.

living-room	....	dining-room	....	bedroom	....
stairs	....	downstairs	....	ceiling	....
toilet	....	floor	....	bathroom	....
cellar	....	upstairs	....	kitchen	....
attic	....	landing	....	hall	....

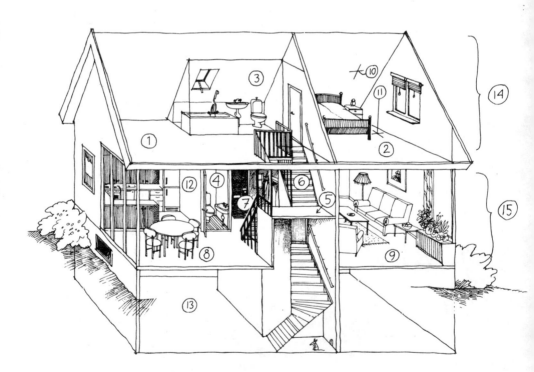

33 Prepositions 3

Fill in the missing prepositions in the following sentences:

1 I met my husband .... a party.
  a on   b by   c at

2 Sally has been a teacher .... three years.
  a for   b since   c in

3 Many Swedes are good .... skiing.
  a to   b at   c in

4 I live .... Queen's Road.
  a on   b in   c by

5 Anne is 25-years-old, but she still lives .... her parents.
  a at   b by   c with

6 See you .... Wednesday .... 7 o'clock.
  a on/on b at/at   c on/at

7 We are having a big party .... New Year's Eve.
  a to   b on   c for

8 Shall we go .... the cinema tonight?
  a on   b at   c to

9 I got a tie .... my girlfriend .... Christmas.
  a for/to b by/at   c from/for

10 Shall we ring .... a taxi?
  a for   b after   c to

11 I must introduce you .... my cousin.
  a to   b with   c for

12 Don't eat sweets, they're bad .... your teeth.
  a to   b for   c with

13 I haven't been to the cinema .... years.
  a at   b since   c for

14 Would you like a piece of cake .... your coffee?
  a with   b to   c for

34 Opposites 5: various words

Complete the following sentences with a word that is opposite in meaning to the one in bold type. Choose from the words below (see example):

behind	last	far	after
single	future	unfurnished	nobody
bottom	shallow	hardly ever	worse
country	always	light	adult

1 **Everybody** likes Janet, but .... *nobody* .... likes John.

2 The river is **deep** here, but it's .... over there.

3 I **often** go to the cinema but I .... go to the theatre.

4 Are you **married** or ....?

5 Ophelia **never** gets up before 9.30 so I am not surprised that she is .... late for work.

6 Is your husband **better** now, Mrs Green?
No, I'm afraid he's a lot ....

7 I'll pick up the **heavy** suitcase and you pick up the .... one.

8 Is the cinema **in front of** or .... the bank?

9 I came **first** in the class in English but .... in Geography.

10 Did you meet your wife **before** or .... you left university?

11 The house is **near** the station—not .... from the library.

12 Now that I'm an .... I wish I were a **child** again.

13 Do the exercise at the **top** of page 36 first, then the one at the ....
of page 37.

14 We know what has happened in the **past**, but we can never tell what will happen
in the ....

.15 Are you looking for a **furnished** flat?
No, I'm looking for an .... one, actually.

16 He lives in the **town** in the winter and in the ....
in the summer.

35 In the living-room

Write the numbers 1–16 next to the correct words.

television set	....	sofa	....	clock	....
ashtray	....	magazines	....	coffee table	....
armchair	....	stereo	....	painting	....
plant	....	wallpaper	....	vase of flowers	....
carpet	....	cushion	....		
bookcase	....	fireplace	....		

36 Missing verbs 8

Fill in the missing verbs in the sentences below. (Remember to choose the correct verb tense.) Choose from the following (see example):

build	fetch	feel
kiss	lie down	offer
paint	pay	post
recognise	refuse	smell

1 Do you think you should ...._kiss_......... a girl the first time you go out with her?

2 The man .... to tell the police where he had hidden the money.

3 I think I'll put a jumper on – I .... a bit cold.

4 Could you go and .... Mum from next-door, Susan. She's wanted on the phone.

5 Is it really you, Simon? I'm sorry, but I didn't .... you without your beard.

6 How long did it take you to .... your house?

7 I feel very tired. I think I'll go and .... for a while.

8 Are you sure it's all right to eat this fish? It .... terrible!

9 We spent the whole day .... the bedroom.

10 "How much did he .... you for your car?" "Three hundred pounds."

11 Put your money away, James. I'll .... for this!

12 Could you .... these letters for me, please?

37 What's the matter?

Fill in the missing words under each of the drawings below. Choose from the following:

a headache	toothache	broken his leg
a sore throat	a cold	burnt himself
a stomach ache	a bad cough	been stung
a temperature	measles	pregnant

He's got ....

She's got ....

He's ....

She's ....

She's got .... He's got .... She's ....

He's .... He's got ....

  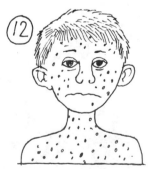

She's got .... He's got .... He's got ....

38 What are they saying? 2

Look at the drawings below and fill in the missing words. Choose from the following:

a Say "Cheese"!

b Have you got the right time, please?

c Drive carefully.

d Would you hold this for me, please?

e Good luck!

f Congratulations!

g Do you mind if I smoke?

h Excuse me, is this seat free?

i What do you do for a living?

j Goodbye. It was nice meeting you.

39 In the kitchen

Write the numbers 1–18 next to the correct words.

sink	....	forks	....	saucers	....
cups	....	glasses	....	dishwasher	....
shelf	....	fridge	....	knives	....
frying pan	....	saucepan	....	tap	....
jug	....	spoons	....	cooker (stove)	....
drawer	....	cupboard	....	plates	....

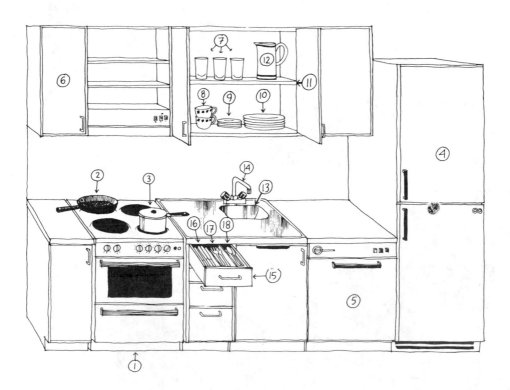

40 Choose the word 3

Fill in the missing word(s) in each of the following sentences:

1 I'm afraid there isn't .... in the car for everyone.

   a space   b room   c places

2 I .... three years ago.

   a stopped smoking   b stopped to smoke   c finished with smoking

3 Excuse me, have you got ...., please?

   a the fire   b a light   c match

4 I like your hat, Julie. It really .... you.

   a passes   b suits   c shows

5 Is there .... for everyone?

   a wine enough   b enough wine   c enough of wine

6 Do you mind if I open the window?

....

   a Yes, of course   b No, of course not   c No, thank you

7 Don't go yet, I'm just going to .... some coffee.

   a make   b cook   c boil

8 I've got a very good .... with the BBC.

   a work   b profession   c job

9 I can't see. Would you .... with me?

   a change places   b change place   c change the place

10 The .... from London to Edinburgh was very tiring.

   a travel   b crossing   c journey

11 I am .... my wife to drive.

   a learning   b teaching   c showing

.... at the party on Saturday.

12 a We were 14 people   b There were 14 of us   c We were 14

I think we've missed the bus.

13 Oh, ... That was the last one.

   a I don't hope so   b I hope we don't   c I hope not

41 Irregular verbs crossword 1

Complete the crossword by filling in the past tense of the verbs in the sentences below (see example):

ACROSS

1	My sister . . . married on April 26th 1980.	GET
2	David . . . very well at the party.	SING
3	He slipped on a banana skin and . . . his leg.	BREAK
4	Do you know who . . . the book 'How Green was my Valley'?	WRITE
5	I was late, so I . . . all the way.	RUN
6	He . . . off a wall and hurt himself.	FALL
7	My cousin . . . for Great Britain in the Olympic Games when he was only 16.	SWIM
8	I . . . three rabbits last weekend.	SHOOT
9	We . . . to Spain last summer.	FLY
10	Who . . . you to play the guitar, Sally?	TEACH

DOWN

a	I'm sorry, but I . . . to post that letter you gave me.	FORGET
b	He . . . the ball to me.	THROW
c	It was cold, so he . . . the window.	SHUT
d	I . . . a whole bottle of champagne on my last birthday.	DRINK
e	A police car . . . me on the motorway.	OVERTAKE
f	I . . . a very interesting book last weekend.	READ
g	I . . . until 11 o'clock this morning.	SLEEP
h	We had a lovely time in Greece. The weather was really beautiful. In fact, the sun . . . all the time.	SHINE
i	I . . . ill this morning so I decided not to go to work.	FEEL
j	A dog . . . her as she was walking through the park	BITE

42 Sports and pastimes 1

Write the number of each drawing next to the correct word.

table tennis	....	skiing	....	painting	....
billiards	....	chess	....	pottery	....
ice hockey	....	sailing	....	cycling	....
football	....	athletics	....	photography	....

43 Sports and pastimes 2

Write the number of each drawing next to the correct word.

stamp collecting	....	dressmaking	....	gardening	....
wrestling	....	skating	....	roller-skating	....
tennis	....	jogging	....	fishing	....
golf	....	show jumping	....	playing cricket	....

44 In the town

Write the number of each drawing next to the correct word(s).

traffic lights	....	church	....
pedestrian crossing	....	bridge	....
pavement	....	police station	....
fire station	....	car park	....
bus stop	....	hospital	....
railway station	....	school	....

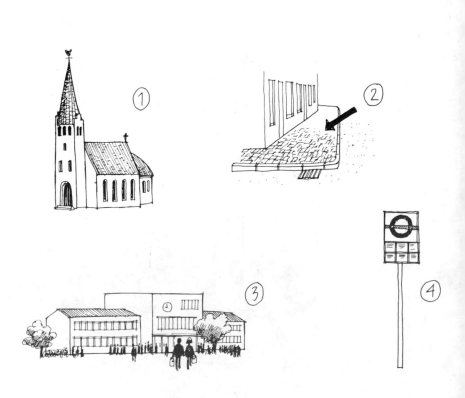

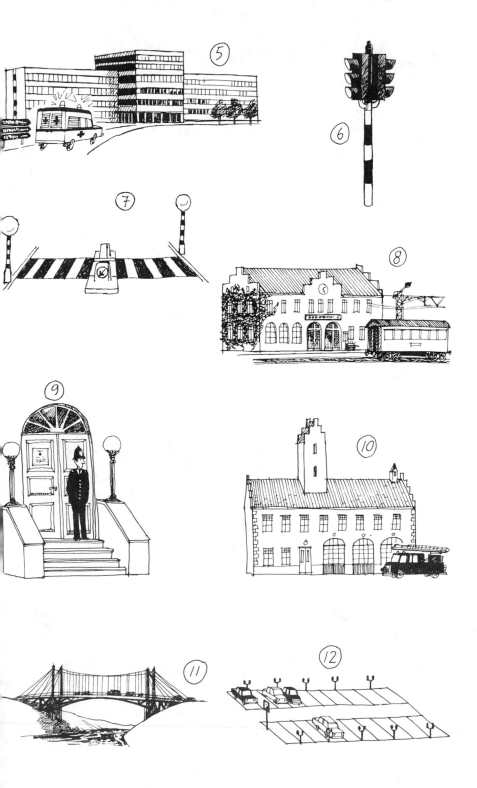

45 Who's saying what?

Below are ten typical phrases used in certain situations. Look at the drawings then decide where each phrase is most likely to be heard. Mark a–j in the bubbles (see example):

a Three gallons of Super, please.
b Any more fares, please?
c Are you being served?
d Could I have the bill, please?
e A second-class single to Man-chester, please.
f Do you take milk and sugar?
g Anything to declare?
h A pound of sugar, please.
i Keep the change!
j Time, gentlemen, please!

46 Jobs in the home

Write the number of each drawing next to the correct word(s).

to darn	....	to do the ironing	....	to make the beds	....
to bake	....	to decorate	....	to clean the windows	....
to dust	....	to do the washing-up	....	to do the washing	....
to tidy up	....	to sweep	....	to do the gardening	....
to polish	....	to vacuum (hoover)	....	to lay the table	....

47 Irregular verbs crossword 2

Complete the crossword by filling in the past tense of the verbs in the sentences below (see example):

ACROSS

1. It was so cold last November that the canal ...   FREEZE
2. The police finally ... the bank robbers after chasing them
   for several hours.   CATCH
3. I ... up at 6.30 this morning.   WAKE
4. Mr and Mrs Brown ... from London to Manchester last
   weekend.   DRIVE
5. The child ... his mother's hand as they crossed the road.   HOLD
6. We ... in the park all afternoon.   SIT
7. We ... up at least fifty balloons for the party.   BLOW
8. My parents ... £35,000 for their house.   PAY
9. He was so tired that he ... down for a while on the bed.   LIE
10. Björn Borg ... the ball into the net.   HIT

DOWN

a She ... a long, white evening-dress to the party.   WEAR
b I ... a £5 note on my way to work this morning.   FIND
c We ... English all the time when we were on holiday.   SPEAK
d He ... his wife at a disco.   MEET
e The child ... her finger while playing with a knife.   CUT
f The thieves ... in the doorway until the police had gone
  past.   HIDE
g He ... his girlfriend a ring for her birthday.   BUY
h The teacher ... a map of Spain on the blackboard.   DRAW
i My cousin ... an actor in 1964.   BECOME
j I thought you ... you would help me.   SAY
k My brother ... his boat himself.   BUILD

48 Prepositions 4

Fill in the missing prepositions in the following sentences:

1 How often do you borrow books .... the library?
   a in   b off   c from

2 Yes, you're right, Jane. I agree .... you.
   a to   b with   c on

3 Cheers! Let's drink .... your success.
   a to   b with   c at

4 Can you look .... the children tonight? I have to go to a meeting.
   a at   b after   c for

5 My children are looking forward .... Christmas.
   a with   b to   c against

6 My brother is living .... a French girl.
   a at   b by   c with

7 Look at the exercise .... the bottom of page 17.
   a on   b at   c in

8 We went to Swansea .... train.
   a by   b with   c on

9 Do you usually have a party .... your birthday?
   a at   b with   c on

10 He put a ladder up .... the wall.
   a to   b against   c on

11 I'm really longing .... the holidays.
   a for   b after   c to

12 What time did you arrive .... London?
   a at   b in   c to

13 There is a bus stop .... the end of the road.
   a at   b in   c to

14 My sister is afraid .... dogs.
   a for   b of   c with

49 Word association

Write next to each of the words on the left a word that is connected with it in some way. Choose from the ones on the right. Use each word **once** only (see example):

1 house	*family*	motorway
2 businessman		wife
3 apple pie		toothache
4 cigarettes		chimney
5 bird		cloud
6 letter		family
7 car		custard
8 school		typewriter
9 husband		comb
10 secretary		saucer
11 tree		nest
12 hair		bridge
13 dentist		trunk
14 cup		library
15 roof		lighter
16 book		train
17 railway station		briefcase
18 river		envelope
19 sky		fork
20 knife		pupils

50 Animals, pets, etc.

Write the number of each drawing next to the correct word.

a dog	a sheep	a duck	a mouse ....
a cat	a goat	a goose	a worm ....
a horse	a chick	a rabbit	a rat ....
a cow	a turkey	a kitten	a frog ....
a pig	a bull	a budgie	a spider ....

Answers

TEST 1

1	sing
2	sleep
3	swim
4	listen
5	drive
6	dance
7	cry
8	write
9	laugh
10	drink
11	read
12	run

TEST 2

1	bad
2	thin
3	small
4	short
5	empty
6	old
7	closed
8	dry
9	cold
10	new
11	sad
12	slow
13	low
14	poor
15	soft

TEST 3

eye	4
mouth	9
tongue	12
hair	1
eyelash	5
forehead	2
chin	14
ear	6
cheek	13
jaw	15
nose	7

eyebrow	3
lip	10
teeth	11
freckles	8

TEST 4

1	between
2	inside
3	on
4	opposite
5	behind
6	over
7	under
8	in front of
9	in
10	next to
11	outside
12	through

TEST 5

1	open
2	fly
3	phone
4	watch
5	learn
6	smoke
7	carry
8	sit down
9	wash
10	ask
11	play
12	eat

TEST 6

arm	5
toe	15
chest	7
head	1
back	4
shoulder	3
foot	14
finger	9
elbow	6

hip	11
knee	13
hand	8
neck	2
leg	12
buttocks/backside	10

TEST 7

1	come
2	know
3	walk
4	tell
5	wear
6	spell
7	Shut
8	climb
9	sell
10	forget
11	cook
12	lose

TEST 8

1	wrong
2	weak
3	alive
4	late
5	thin
6	narrow
7	female
8	unkind
9	stupid
10	dirty
11	expensive
12	difficult
13	unfriendly
14	noisy
15	awake

TEST 9

Down

1	Britain
2	Italy
3	Swedish

4 Holland
5 Chinese
6 Greek
7 Germany
8 Denmark
9 American

Across

1 Switzerland
2 Poland
3 French
4 Indian
5 Norwegian
6 Russian
7 Spain

TEST 10

a postman	4
a policeman	9
a shop assistant	1
a waiter	5
an electrician	2
a typist	7
a secretary	10
a doctor	8
a nurse	3
a dentist	6

TEST 11

1 finishes
2 hear
3 leave
4 speaks
5 look at
6 count
7 cut
8 copies
9 help
10 draws
11 Follow
12 understand

TEST 12

1 some
2 can speak
3 was born
4 is

5 tall
6 far
7 of mine
8 Everyone
9 get up
10 ill (sick = American English)
11 use
12 tell
13 any
14 I'm sorry

TEST 13

an actress	8
a bus driver	1
a fireman	7
an optician	5
a hairdresser	3
an office worker	9
an engineer	2
a businesswoman	10
a mechanic	4
a bank clerk	6

TEST 14

1 It's sunny
2 It's frosty
3 It's foggy
4 It's raining
5 It's thawing
6 It's cloudy
7 It's clearing up
8 It's windy
9 It's freezing
10 It's snowing

TEST 15

1 is ('s) knocking
2 pronounce
3 is ('s) shining
4 causes
5 stay
6 marry
7 is ('s) choosing
8 lies
9 delivers
10 wait

11 am ('m) making
12 am ('m) dreaming

TEST 16

Down

1 cities
2 buses
3 women
4 glasses
5 leaves
6 teeth
7 ladies

Across

1 mice
2 potatoes
3 children
4 geese
5 feet
6 days
7 men
8 knives
9 boxes

TEST 17

a cup of tea	5
vegetables	9
an ice-cream	12
jam	6
a banana	1
bread	8
wine	11
sausages	4
oranges	2
toast	7
bacon and eggs	3
cheese	10

TEST 18

1 to start
2 to cry
3 to close
4 to go
5 to play
6 to take
7 to teach
8 to borrow

9   to turn off
10 to answer
11 to dislike
12 to buy
13 to push
14 to stand up
15 to depart

TEST 19

1 at
2 on
3 for
4 at ... in
5 at
6 on
7 at
8 in
9 since
10 in
11 for ... in
12 in
13 on
14 for
15 since

TEST 20

1 A box of matches,
   please.
2 After you!
3 Bless you!
4 Oh, sorry!
5 Excuse me, please.
6 Do sit down.
7 Cheers!
8 Help yourselves.
9 How do you do.
10 Look out!

TEST 21

1 need
2 cleaned
3 moved
4 cost
5 dresses
6 jumped
7 describe
8 continue

9 want
10 enjoyed
11 rained
12 talk

TEST 22

tomatoes   5
a cup of coffee   9
butter   12
meat   2
soup   7
beer   10
pears   4
a boiled egg   1
a cake   11
potatoes   6
apples   3
biscuits   8

TEST 23

1 There's
2 am going
3 work
4 Pass
5 well
6 people
7 back
8 with
9 comes with
10 a swim
11 That's all right
12 such
13 a loaf of bread
14 nice

TEST 24

1 Today
2 tomorrow
3 yesterday
4 next Thursday
5 tonight
6 the day after tomorrow
7 tomorrow afternoon
8 last Thursday
9 this afternoon
10 last night

11 this morning
12 the day before yesterday

TEST 25

nuts   9
beans   4
a sandwich   8
a hot dog   12
a grapefruit   1
crispbread   5
crayfish   10
chicken   2
spaghetti   11
Danish pastries   7
fish and chips   3
a glass of milk   6

TEST 26

1 to hate
2 to fall asleep
3 to die
4 to suck
5 to go to bed
6 to save
7 to mend
8 to whisper
9 to lose
10 to feel well
11 to find
12 to hide
13 to forget
14 to take off
15 to sink

TEST 27

1 happy
2 hot
3 comfortable
4 frightened
5 cold
6 tired
7 sad
8 correct
9 embarrassed
10 nervous
11 ill
12 worried

TEST 28

Missing words:
- Yes, please. I'm looking for a jumper.
- Er ... size 38, I think.
- Yes. Blue, if possible.
- Yes, that looks nice. How much is it?
- Yes, please.
- I see. Thank you.
- Yes, it was perfect. I'll take it.
- Thank you. Now, where's my purse ...

TEST 29

door	7
gate	11
roof	1
garden	9
garage	8
chimney	2
hedge	12
wall	4
path	10
drainpipe	5
window	6
balcony	3

TEST 30

1 baked
2 have ('ve) quarrelled
3 failed
4 have decided
5 studied
6 have promised
7 explained
8 joined
9 happened
10 combed
11 agreed
12 demanded

TEST 31

1 shoe shop
2 chemist's
3 fishmonger's
4 butcher's
5 barber's
6 greengrocer's
7 grocer's
8 off-licence
9 florist's
10 newsagent's
11 tobacconist's
12 baker's
13 post office
14 hairdresser's
15 furniture shop
16 boutique
17 jeweller's
18 dry-cleaner's
19 ironmonger's
20 optician's
21 bank
22 launderette
23 café
24 travel agency
25 stationer's

TEST 32

living-room	9
stairs	6
toilet	4
cellar	13
attic	1
dining-room	8
downstairs	15
floor	11
upstairs	14
landing	5
bedroom	2
ceiling	10
bathroom	3
kitchen	12
hall	7

TEST 33

1 at
2 for
3 at
4 in
5 with
6 on/at
7 on
8 to
9 from/for
10 for
11 to
12 for
13 for
14 with

TEST 34

1 nobody
2 shallow
3 hardly ever
4 single
5 always
6 worse
7 light
8 behind
9 last
10 after
11 far
12 adult
13 bottom
14 future
15 unfurnished
16 country

TEST 35

television set	4
ashtray	7
armchair	10
plant	16
carpet	13
bookcase	1
sofa	5
magazines	8
stereo	2
wallpaper	14
cushion	11
fireplace	3
clock	15
coffee table	6
painting	12
vase of flowers	9

TEST 36

1 kiss
2 refused
3 feel/am feeling
4 fetch
5 recognise
6 build
7 lie down
8 smells
9 painting
10 offer
11 pay
12 post

TEST 37

1 toothache
2 a headache
3 broken his leg
4 been stung
5 a cold
6 a sore throat
7 pregnant
8 burnt himself
9 a bad cough
10 a temperature
11 a stomach ache
12 measles

TEST 38

1 Congratulations!
2 Excuse me, is this seat free?
3 Would you hold this for me, please?
4 Do you mind if I smoke?
5 Drive carefully!
6 Say "Cheese"!
7 Have you got the right time, please?
8 Good luck!
9 Goodbye. It was nice meeting you.
10 What do you do for a living?

TEST 39

sink	13
cups	8
shelf	11
frying pan	2
jug	12
drawer	15
forks	17
glasses	7
fridge	4
saucepan	3
spoons	18
cupboard	6
saucers	9
dishwasher	5
knives	16
tap	14
cooker (stove)	1
plates	10

TEST 40

1 room
2 stopped smoking
3 a light
4 suits
5 enough wine
6 No, of course not
7 make
8 job
9 change places
10 journey
11 teaching
12 There were 14 of us
13 I hope not

TEST 41

Across
1 got
2 sang
3 broke
4 wrote
5 ran
6 fell
7 swam
8 shot
9 flew
10 taught

Down
a forgot
b threw
c shut
d drank
e overtook
f read
g slept
h shone
i felt
j bit

TEST 42

table tennis	6
billiards	3
ice hockey	8
football	1
skiing	10
chess	5
sailing	4
athletics	9
painting	7
pottery	2
cycling	11
photography	12

TEST 43

stamp collecting	4
wrestling	10
tennis	2
golf	7
dressmaking	6
skating	11
jogging	9
show jumping	3
gardening	8
roller-skating	5
fishing	1
playing cricket	12

TEST 44

traffic lights	6
pedestrian crossing	7
pavement	2
fire station	10
bus stop	4
railway station	8

church	1
bridge	11
police station	9
car park	12
hospital	5
school	3

TEST 45

1	e
2	a
3	h
4	d
5	i
6	b
7	j
8	c
9	g
10	f

TEST 46

to darn	7
to bake	5
to dust	2
to tidy up	15
to polish	6
to do the ironing	11
to decorate	1
to do the washing-up	10
to sweep	13
to vacuum (hoover)	8
to make the beds	3
to clean the windows	9
to do the washing	12
to do the gardening	4
to lay the table	14

TEST 47

Across

1	froze
2	caught
3	woke
4	drove
5	held
6	sat
7	blew
8	paid
9	lay
10	hit

Down

a	wore
b	found
c	spoke
d	met
e	cut
f	hid
g	bought
h	drew
i	became
j	said
k	built

TEST 48

1	from
2	with
3	to
4	after
5	to
6	with
7	at
8	by
9	on
10	against
11	for
12	in
13	at
14	of

TEST 49

1	family
2	briefcase
3	custard
4	lighter
5	nest
6	envelope
7	motorway
8	pupils
9	wife
10	typewriter
11	trunk
12	comb
13	toothache
14	saucer
15	chimney
16	library
17	train
18	bridge
19	cloud
20	fork

TEST 50

a dog	6
a cat	10
a horse	18
a cow	2
a pig	13
a sheep	17
a goat	19
a chick	1
a turkey	14
a bull	7
a duck	3
a goose	16
a rabbit	9
a kitten	12
a budgie	5
a mouse	8
a worm	20
a rat	4
a frog	15
a spider	11